A TRUE BOOK™

W9-BKL-728

SPACE EXPLORATION

THE INTERNATIONAL
SPACE
STATION

Rebecca Kraft Rector

Children's Press®
An imprint of Scholastic Inc.

Content Consultant
Roger D. Launius, PhD
Former Chief Historian, NASA

SAFETY NOTE

Safety note! The activity suggested on pages 42 to 43 of this book should be done with adult supervision. Observe safety and caution at all times. The author and publisher disclaim all liability for any damage, mishap, or injury that may occur from engaging in the activity featured in this book.

Library of Congress Cataloging-in-Publication Data

Names: Rector, Rebecca Kraft, author.

Title: The International Space Station/Rebecca Kraft Rector.

Other titles: True book.

Description: First edition. | New York: Children's Press, an imprint of Scholastic, Inc., 2022. | Series: A true book | Includes bibliographical references and index. | Audience: Ages 8–10. | Audience: Grades 4–6. | Summary: "A new set of True Books on Space Exploration"— Provided by publisher.

Identifiers: LCCN 2021041600 (print) | LCCN 2021041601 (ebook) | ISBN 9781338825220 (library binding) | ISBN 9781338825510 (paperback) | ISBN 9781338825879 (ebk)

Subjects: LCSH: International Space Station—Juvenile literature. | Space stations—Juvenile literature. | Outer space—Exploration—Juvenile literature.

Classification: LCC TL797.15 .R43 2022 (print) | LCC TL797.15 (ebook) | DDC 629.44/2—dc23

LC record available at https://lccn.loc.gov/2021041600

LC ebook record available at https://lccn.loc.gov/2021041601

Copyright © 2022 by Scholastic Inc.

All rights reserved. Published by Children's Press, an imprint of Scholastic Inc., *Publishers since 1920.* SCHOLASTIC, CHILDREN'S PRESS, TRUE BOOKS™, and associated logos are trademarks and/or registered trademarks of Scholastic Inc.

The publisher does not have any control over and does not assume any responsibility for author or third-party websites or their content.

No part of this publication may be reproduced, stored in a retrieval system, or transmitted in any form or by any means, electronic, mechanical, photocopying, recording, or otherwise, without written permission of the publisher. For information regarding permission, write to Scholastic Inc., Attention: Permissions Department, 557 Broadway, New York, NY 10012.

10 9 8 7 6 5 4 3 2 1   22 23 24 25 26

Printed in the U.S.A. 113

First edition, 2022

Design by Kathleen Petelinsek

Series produced by Spooky Cheetah Press

Front cover: The ISS in its orbit of Earth

Back cover: An ISS astronaut exercising

Find the Truth!

Everything you are about to read is true *except* for one of the sentences on this page.

Which one is **TRUE**?

T or F   There's a copy of the International Space Station in a swimming pool.

T or F   It's very quiet inside the International Space Station.

Find the answers in this book.

What's in This Book?

Introduction **6**

1 Assembling the ISS
How do you build a laboratory in space? **9**

2 ISS Astronauts
What does it take to be chosen for
the astronaut program? **17**

3 Daily Life in Outer Space
What's it like to live and work in orbit? **23**

Playing music is one way astronauts relax.

Astronauts training

The **BIG** Truth

How Does Living in Space Affect Our Bodies?

What did NASA's twin study show about how space travel affects humans? **32**

4 Outer Space Experiments

What experiments does the crew work on? **35**

Think Like a Scientist **40**
Activity: Fluid Shift **42**
True Statistics **44**
Resources **45**
Glossary **46**
Index **47**
About the Author **48**

Testing peppers grown in space

Out of This World!

There is a **science laboratory** in outer space called the **International Space Station** (ISS). For more than 20 years, it has **orbited** our planet and hosted crews from around the world. Working on the ISS isn't easy. **Astronauts float** around inside the ISS as if they were weightless. In fact, **everything floats!**

Still, the ISS crew has managed to conduct more than **3,000 science experiments**. They are trying to find out what happens to plants, animals, materials, and people **in space**.

The International Space Station is a remarkable feat of science and engineering. It's the result of countries around the world **working together** for an out-of-this-world goal—enabling humans to **live and work in space!**

Zarya means "sunrise" in the Russian language.

Zarya provided electrical power, storage, propulsion, and guidance to the ISS during its initial assembly.

Assembling the ISS

The National Aeronautics and Space Administration (NASA) is the space agency of the United States. Experts from NASA worked with countries from around the world to build the International Space Station. It wasn't easy!

The station couldn't be built all at once. It had to be assembled in pieces, called **modules**, over many years. Every piece had to be sent into space on rockets. Russia launched the first module, Zarya, on November 20, 1998.

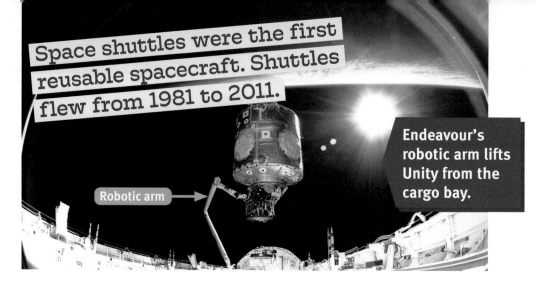

Space shuttles were the first reusable spacecraft. Shuttles flew from 1981 to 2011.

Robotic arm

Endeavour's robotic arm lifts Unity from the cargo bay.

Placing Unity

Space shuttles played an important part in building the ISS. They carried crew and equipment back and forth. In December 1998, the space shuttle Endeavour carried the next module, Unity, into space. Unity is a passageway that has several **docking** spaces. Docking spaces enable spacecraft to connect to the passageway. To connect Unity to Zarya, Endeavour's commander, Bob Cabana, had to meet Zarya in its orbit. Astronaut Nancy Currie operated Endeavour's robotic arm to place the module.

Let's Get Building!

Time for a spacewalk! Or, as astronauts call it, an EVA—extravehicular activity. Put on your spacesuit so you'll have drinking water and oxygen. You could be working in space for hours! Exit through the airlock and be sure your tethers are connected to the spacecraft. You don't want to float away. But if you do—don't panic. You're wearing the SAFER (a Simplified Aid for EVA Rescue) like a backpack. You can use the joystick and fire the jets to get back "home" again. Make sure your tools are tethered to your spacesuit. Ready? Then get to work. That space station won't build itself!

Astronauts Robert L. Curbeam, Jr. (left) and Christer Fuglesang at work on the ISS

A Place to Live

The next module, Zvezda, was launched in July 2000. It provided living space, small windows, and life support systems—so the crew doesn't need to wear spacesuits inside. Among other things, life support means air to breathe—provided by oxygen tanks that were brought from Earth. The life support equipment also controls temperature inside the station. In November 2000, the first crew of three astronauts could move onto the ISS. A few weeks later, two solar panels were added to the ISS.

The solar panels on the ISS convert sunlight into electricity.

Astronauts Carlos Noriega (left) and Joe Tanner work on the ISS's solar array.

Astronaut Meg McArthur reads a book in Cupola.

Expanding the ISS

Over time, more living spaces and life support systems were added. The United States, the European Space Agency, and Japan each added a lab as well. By 2007, the station was ready for three more crew members to move in, for a total of six. More docking spaces were added, plus a module called Cupola. Cupola's seven big windows make it easier for the crew to observe and direct outside operations, such as spacewalks, docking, and use of the robotic arm.

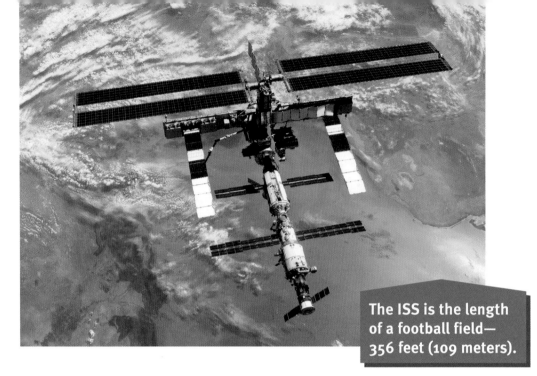

The ISS is the length of a football field— 356 feet (109 meters).

Assembly Complete! . . . Sort of

In 2011, construction of the ISS was considered complete. However, improvements continue to be made. In 2016, the Bigelow Expandable Activity Module (BEAM) was delivered. It is being used for storage space. The Russian lab module Nauka arrived in 2021. By the end of 2023, six new pairs of solar arrays will be completely installed. The new arrays are half the size of the old ones and twice as powerful.

Spotting the Space Station

You can see the ISS from Earth—without a telescope! It looks like a bright spot moving quickly, high in the night sky. That light you see is the sun's light reflecting off the ISS. The station may be visible only for a few minutes at a time, though, because it moves so fast. The ISS travels five miles per second. That's the same as 18,000 miles per hour! For comparison, cars drive about 60 miles per hour on the highway.

The ISS orbits Earth 16 times a day.

ISS path

The NASA website has a map showing when the ISS will pass your area.

Astronauts on Expedition 61 dressed up for Halloween!

Russian astronauts are called cosmonauts. Chinese astronauts are called taikonauts.

ISS Astronauts

The first crew of three astronauts arrived on the ISS on November 2, 2000. Since then there have always been people on the station. There is usually a six-member crew for each mission, and they ordinarily stay for six months. When a group of three leaves, three new astronauts come on board. Each time the crew changes, the six-person crew is given a new Expedition number and a mission patch for their flight suits.

Tough Training

The NASA astronaut training program accepts applicants about every four years. Thousands of scientists and engineers apply, but fewer than ten might be chosen each time. Basic training takes about two years. Trainees study many subjects and learn skills they'll need later. To learn how to work in spacesuits, trainees practice underwater! NASA even has a full-size mock-up, or copy, of the ISS in a huge swimming pool. Astronauts also use virtual reality headsets for training.

Trainees practice equipment repair and other tasks in the pool.

Moving through water is similar to moving in outer space.

British astronaut Tim Peake said learning Russian was the toughest part of training!

When needed, astronauts hook their feet to bars or cables to keep from floating away!

Learning a New Language

NASA astronauts who travel to the International Space Station must also learn to speak Russian. They need to be able to communicate with the Russian-speaking team at Mission Control in Moscow, Russia. Crew members from outside the United States must also know how to speak English in addition to Russian. It's essential that everyone on the station be able to understand one another, especially in emergencies.

The ISS Crew

Each ISS crew member has a title and a special responsibility. The commander is in charge of the station. The commander makes sure all crew stay safe and do their jobs well. Flight engineers look after the spacecraft and all its systems, such as life support and electrical. The science officer is in charge of the ISS science experiments. Although each has a specialty, every crew member must be ready to do any job that is needed.

Joan Higginbotham is the third Black woman to go to space. Mae Jemison was the first.

Astronauts Joan E. Higginbotham (right) and Sunita L. Williams at the controls of one of the station's robotic arms

Tourists Visit the ISS

Millionaire Dennis Tito was the first-ever space tourist! In April 2001, he launched in a Russian Soyuz rocket and spent eight days on the ISS. Seven more tourists visited the ISS, but tourism stopped in 2009. Then, in 2019, NASA said it would allow two civilians per year to travel in a U.S. commercial spacecraft to visit the ISS. Visitors would be doing experiments and other NASA-approved activities. But this trip isn't for everyone. The cost of the visit is $35,000 a day—and that's after you've paid to get to the station. The flight aboard a SpaceX or Boeing rocket can cost 50 million dollars!

Dennis Tito

Reid Wiseman (shown here on the ISS) served as the flight engineer for Expedition 41 in 2014.

Ground teams on Earth create the schedules for the ISS astronauts.

CHAPTER 3

Daily Life in Outer Space

On Earth each day and night lasts for 24 hours, but that's not true in space, especially on the ISS. The station's fast orbit around Earth means the ISS crew sees the sun rise 16 times in 24 hours! But our bodies are used to an Earth pattern of waking and sleeping, so ISS astronauts stick to a 24-hour schedule. The ISS crew is normally on a rotation of 12 hours working and 12 hours off.

Trash leaves the ISS in an uncrewed spacecraft. Everything burns up when the ship enters Earth's atmosphere.

A vacuum attachment collects clippings during haircuts.

Getting Ready for the Day

Morning routines are tricky in **microgravity**! Astronauts wash with wet towels and no-rinse soap, then put on **disposable** clothing. There are no washers and dryers on the ISS! After brushing their teeth, the astronauts have to spit into paper towels. When it's time to use the toilet, they grip bars to hold themselves down. The astronauts' urine is collected and purified for drinking. A powerful fan carries solid waste through a suction hole. Later, it goes out with the rest of the trash.

Hard at Work

The crew is always busy. The astronauts work on science experiments and participate in medical experiments that show how their bodies react to living in microgravity. Crew members also need to take care of the station. If there is a leak, for example, crew members need to repair it. It's also important to keep the ISS clean. Crew members wash walls, floors, and windows; clean filters; and vacuum.

Cleaning the space toilet is all part of the job on the ISS!

Let's Eat!

As with everything else in microgravity, mealtimes are a challenge. Astronauts use tortillas instead of bread to keep floating crumbs to a minimum. Thick foods like pudding are easy to eat because they stick to the spoons. But astronauts use straws to sip soups and drinks from bags. Utensils are magnetized or stuck down with Velcro when no one's using them. And everything is cleaned with germ-killing wipes, since there's no water to spare.

Salt and pepper have to be liquid because grains would float away.

Astronauts can choose from a variety of foods, including fruit, peanut butter, chicken, beef, and seafood. Pizza is a special treat.

> Astronauts posed with one of their cookies in a pouch.

Space Cookies!

In November 2019, a zero-**gravity** oven arrived on the ISS. It was specially designed to work in microgravity. The oven was an experiment to see if food could be baked in space. So what was the first thing the astronauts baked? Chocolate chip cookies, of course! The cookie dough came in a special pouch to keep in the crumbs, and only one cookie could be baked at a time. The crew said the cookies smelled delicious. Unfortunately, they weren't allowed to eat them. The baked cookies returned to Earth to be tested by scientists. They are investigating how microgravity affects food baked from raw ingredients.

Astronauts maintain a fitness regimen before, during, and after their flight.

Harness

Keeping Strong

Astronauts living in microgravity exercise up to three hours every day to keep their bones and muscles strong. To run on a treadmill, crew members wear a harness that keeps them from floating away. They also ride an exercise bike and use a **resistance** machine that works like lifting weights to keep their muscles strong. During her mission on the ISS, Sunita Williams ran the 2007 Boston Marathon on the onboard treadmill.

Let's Relax

Astronauts on the ISS are away from their families and friends—and their planet—for a long time. Outside the station, there's harmful **radiation**, extremely hot or cold temperatures, and no air. The stress of having such a dangerous job could easily become overwhelming. To relax, astronauts stay in touch with family through email and video calls, take pictures of one another, and keep up with their hobbies—like reading or watching movies.

One group of astronauts formed a rock band in space!

Astronaut Jessica Meir relaxes by playing the saxophone.

29

Staying Connected

Astronauts aren't left alone in space. They're always in touch with the Mission Control Centers on Earth. Astronauts also speak with classroom students through the Ask an Astronaut program and through Amateur Radio on the International Space Station (ARISS). You might think there would be a delay for the astronauts' words to reach Earth. But communication moves quickly through **satellites** in orbit to antennas on the ground, so delays are not a problem.

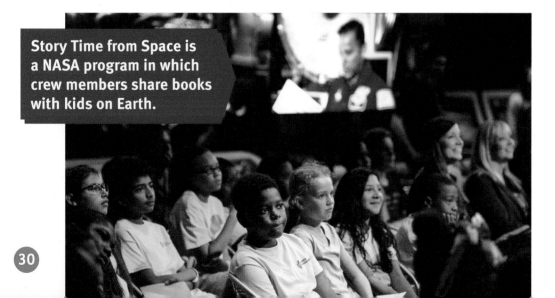

Story Time from Space is a NASA program in which crew members share books with kids on Earth.

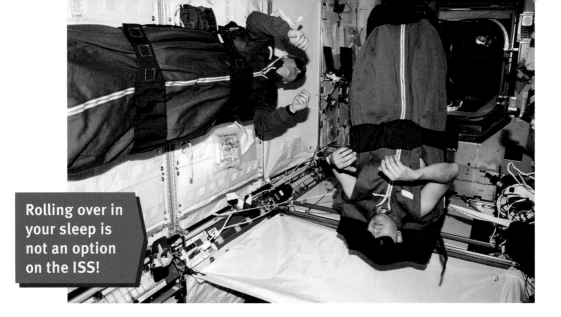

Rolling over in your sleep is not an option on the ISS!

Sleeping Upside Down

When the schedule says it's time for their eight hours of sleep, the crew members hook their sleeping bags to the wall. The astronauts sleep in bags so they don't float around, but they can sleep in any position they want. The body doesn't care about directions in microgravity. There is no real right side up and upside down. There is a lot of noise, though. Some astronauts wear earplugs because of the noise from the fans and filters. They say it's like living inside a giant vacuum cleaner.

How Does Living in Space Affect Our Bodies?

Mark

Scott

Human beings have been to the moon—and now we're thinking about traveling to Mars. But hold on! Scientists don't know if our bodies can handle living in space for long periods of time. NASA had a chance to gather information with a study of twins. They compared identical twin astronauts Scott and Mark Kelly. Identical twins share many characteristics, right down to their genes! Scott stayed on the ISS for a year while Mark remained on Earth. Check out how Scott's body changed in microgravity.

Height

There was no direct gravity pulling Scott's body down on the ISS, so his spine got slightly longer in space. He was a little taller when he returned home.

Scott

Eyesight

In microgravity, **fluids** shift in the body. Astronauts' faces get puffy, and their legs get skinnier. The fluids moving to Scott's upper body also caused his eyeballs to change shape and his eyesight to worsen.

Mark

Aging Process

Scientists examined Scott's telomeres, which are a part of his chromosomes. As people get older, their telomeres grow shorter. Scott's telomeres grew longer in space!

Mark's body did not show any of the changes that Scott's had shown while he was in space. And Scott's height, sight, and telomeres all returned to normal when he came back to Earth!

Many fields of study are researched on the ISS. These include biology, earth science, physical science, and technology.

Astronauts stow research samples in a freezer.

CHAPTER

Outer Space Experiments

The ISS provides a unique opportunity for research in many fields of study. Scientists at the station experiment with plants and animals (including people), trying to identify the effects microgravity has on them. Sometimes scientists leave the station and step into outer space to study the effects of radiation, vacuum (empty space where there's no air), and extreme temperatures on different materials or spacecraft equipment.

Astronauts ate the first salad made from lettuce grown in space on August 10, 2015.

Plant experiments on the ISS are done in special growth chambers.

Growing Food for the Future

Supply ships deliver food to astronauts on the ISS. But for humans to travel to Mars, we need to learn to grow food in microgravity. Scientists hope to produce nutritious plants that also taste good. The crops can't take up a lot of room and must be able to resist diseases. Plant experiments on the ISS are monitored by the astronauts and by researchers on Earth. The astronauts have grown peas, radishes, and soybeans. They've also grown leafy greens, such as mustard and pak choi.

Spicing It Up

In 2021, scientists sent chili pepper seeds to the ISS. Growing the peppers would be the most complex project to date. Chili peppers take four months from sprouting to harvesting. And the flowers must be **pollinated** before they can produce peppers. But there are no bees on the ISS, so the crew had to pollinate the flowers by hand. Peppers have several features to recommend them as food for space. First, they're spicy. Astronauts lose some of their sense of taste in microgravity, so spices can make food taste better. Second, peppers are full of vitamin C, so they are nutritious. Third, they're bright red and green. Growing colorful foods can lift the astronauts' spirits and improve their well-being. Some of the peppers were sent back to Earth so they can be tested to see if they are safe to eat.

Peppers grown on the ISS are gathered for testing on Earth.

A Global Effort

One of the greatest accomplishments of this out-of-this-world project is the international cooperation needed to make it work. Sixteen nations work together on the ISS program: the United States, Canada, Japan, Russia, Brazil, and several European nations.

The United States provided two laboratories and a habitation module for the ISS. Two Russian

Timeline of ISS Milestones

NOVEMBER 20, 1998
Russia launches Zarya, the first ISS module.

NOVEMBER 2, 2000
The first crew of two Russians and one American moves onto the ISS.

APRIL 2008
Peggy Whitson becomes the first female ISS commander.

NOVEMBER 24, 2014
The first 3D-printed object in space is created on the ISS—a replacement part for the printer itself!

research modules, one Japanese laboratory, and one European Space Agency (ESA) laboratory are there as well.

The ISS is more than 20 years old. The decades that humans have spent living and researching there have resulted in incredible discoveries. Hopefully, many more advances will come out of it in the future. Only time will tell.

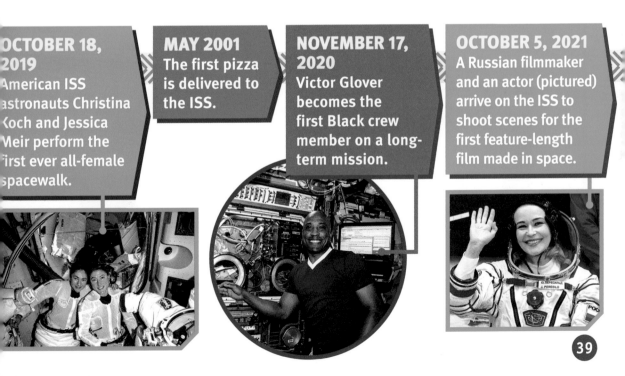

OCTOBER 18, 2019
American ISS astronauts Christina Koch and Jessica Meir perform the first ever all-female spacewalk.

MAY 2001
The first pizza is delivered to the ISS.

NOVEMBER 17, 2020
Victor Glover becomes the first Black crew member on a long-term mission.

OCTOBER 5, 2021
A Russian filmmaker and an actor (pictured) arrive on the ISS to shoot scenes for the first feature-length film made in space.

Tomatoes in Space!

Scientists conduct experiments and study data.

School kids in the Tomatosphere™ program are helping scientists. They conduct tests to see which seeds germinate better on Earth—those that have spent time on the ISS (Type G) or those that haven't (Type H). Study the graph of their results and answer the questions.

Students (right) studied how "space seeds" (left) germinated on Earth.

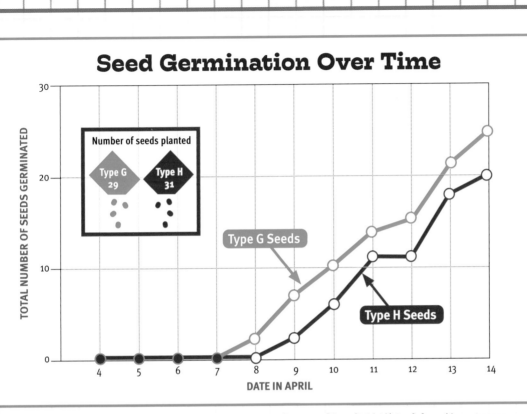

Seed Germination Over Time

Source: Let's Talk Science http://tomatosphere.letstalkscience.ca/Resources/library/ArticleId/5879/infographic-creator.aspx

Analyze It!

1 Which seeds germinated first?

2 Which seeds had the highest percentage of total seeds germinated?

3 What patterns do you see on the graph?

4 What conclusions can you draw from these results?

ANSWERS: 1. Type G, the seeds that had been to the ISS. 2. Type G. 3. After April 8, the germination rate of both seeds went up, but the number of Type G seeds germinated was always greater. 4. Crops (in general) might produce more food if seeds spent time in microgravity before being planted.

Fluid Shift

In microgravity, fluids spread out through the body. As we have seen, astronauts' faces get puffy, and their legs get skinnier. With the help of a partner, you can imitate this fluid shift with this activity.

Materials

Watch or clock

Washable marker or masking tape

Tape measure

Paper and marker for recording data

Directions

1 Stand for 10 minutes. Then ask a partner to use the marker or masking tape to mark three places—A, B, and C—on your bare leg. Above the knee, on the calf, and on the ankle are good spots!

4 Have your partner measure the same spots. Record the data.

2 Ask your partner to measure around your leg at the three marked spots. Record the data.

3 Now lie on the floor with your legs straight up at a 90-degree angle. You can prop them on a wall or chair. Keep your legs up for 10 minutes.

5 Compare the results. What do they tell you?

Explain It!

Using what you learned in the book, can you explain what happened and why? Look back at page 33 if you need help.

Number of countries from which individuals have visited the ISS: 19

Number of orbits the ISS makes in 24 hours: 16

Amount of space the solar arrays cover: A little more than .5 acre (about the size of 10 tennis courts)

Year with most spacewalks from the ISS since its launch: 2007 with 23 spacewalks

Weight of the ISS: About a million pounds (454,000 kilograms)

Total miles of wire connecting the ISS electrical power system: 8

Number of spaceships that can dock at one time: 8

Time it takes the fastest rocket to reach the ISS from Earth: 4 hours

Number of computers controlling the ISS systems: More than 50

Did you find the truth?

T There's a copy of the International Space Station in a swimming pool.

F It's very quiet inside the International Space Station.

Resources

Other books in this series:

 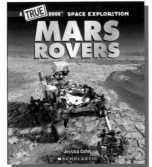 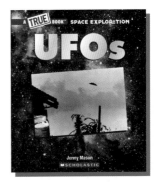

You can also look at:

Gifford, Clive. *International Space Station*. London: Hachette, 2019.

Gregory, Josh. *If You Were a Kid Docking at the International Space Station*. New York: Scholastic, 2018.

McCarthy, Cecilia Pinto. *Engineering the International Space Station*. Minneapolis: Abdo Publishing, 2018.

Glossary

disposable (dis-POH-zuh-buhl) made to be thrown away after use

docking (DAHK-ing) connecting one spacecraft to another

fluid (FLOO-id) a substance that can flow, such as a liquid or a gas

gravity (GRAV-i-tee) the force that pulls things toward the center of Earth and keeps them from floating away

microgravity (mye-kroh-GRAV-i-tee) a condition in space when the pull of gravity is not very strong

modules (MAH-joolz) separate units that can be joined to others to make things such as two parts of a spaceship

orbited (OR-bit-id) traveled in a circular path around something, especially a planet or the sun

pollinated (PAH-luh-nay-tid) the process by which pollen is transferred between flowering plants to create seeds

radiation (ray-dee-AY-shuhn) energy given off in the form of light or heat

resistance (ri-ZIS-tuhns) a force that opposes the motion of an object

satellites (SAT-uh-lites) spacecraft, moons, or other heavenly bodies that travel in an orbit around a larger heavenly body

Index

Page numbers in **bold** indicate illustrations.

Amateur Radio on the International
   Space Station (ARISS), 30
Ask an Astronaut, 30
astronauts
   assembling ISS, 10–11, **10–11**
   effects of living in space, 32–33,
     32–33, 42
   living and working on ISS, 12–13,
     12–13, **16–17**, 17, **22–31**, 23–31,
     34–37, 35–37, **39**
   training for ISS, 18–20, **18–20**

Bigelow Expandable Activity Module
   (BEAM), 14

Cupola module, 13, **13**

docking spaces, 10, **10**, 13

Earth orbit, 15
Endeavour shuttle, 10, **10**
European Space Agency (ESA), 13, 39
extravehicular activity (EVA), 11, **11**

gravity, 27, 33

International Space Station (ISS)
   assembly of, 9–11, **9–11**, 14
   description, 7
   international cooperation, 38–39
   living and working on, 12–13, **12–13**,
     16–17, 17, **22–31**, 23–31, **34–37**,
     35–37, **39**
   milestones timeline, **38–39**

size, **14**
tourist visits, 21, **21**
viewed from Earth, 15, **15**

microgravity, 24–28, 31–33, 35–37, 42
modules, **8**, 9–10, 12–14, **13**, 38–39, **38**

National Aeronautics and Space
   Administration (NASA), 9, 15, 18–19,
   21, 30, **30**, 32
Nauka module, 14

radiation, 29, 35
robotic arms, 10, **10**, 13, **20**

satellites, 30
science experiments, 7, 20–21, 25, 27,
   27, **34–37**, 35–37, 40–43, **40–43**
shuttles, 10, **10**
Simplified Aid for EVA Rescue (SAFER),
   11, **11**
solar panels, 12, **12**, 14, **14**
Soyuz rocket, 21
space cookies, 27, **27**
spacewalks, 11, **11**, 13, **39**
Story Time from Space, **30**

Tito, Dennis, 21, **21**
twins, study of, 32–33, **32–33**

Unity module, 10, **10**

Zarya module, **8**, 9–10, **38**
Zvezda module, 12

About the Author

Rebeca Kraft Rector is the author of more than 30 fiction and nonfiction books for children. After earning a master's degree in library science, she worked for many years as a librarian. She especially enjoyed helping children find the information they needed. Many of Rebecca's nonfiction titles investigate the sciences, including astronomy, Earth, and animals. She has also written two picture books and a science-fiction novel for children. Visit her website at RebeccaKraftRector.wordpress.com.

Photos ©: back cover: Mark T. Vande Hei/NASA; 3, 4, 5 top: NASA; 5 bottom: Ben Smegelsky/NASA; 8, 10, 11: NASA; 12: NASA/AFP/Getty Images; 13, 14: NASA; 15: Stocktrek Images, Inc/Alamy Images; 16–17, 18, 19, 20: NASA; 21 inset: Newsmakers/Getty Images; 22–23: NASA; 24: ESA/NASA; 25: NASA; 26: NASA/AP Images; 27 inset: Twitter/Astro_Christina/NASA; 28: Mark T. Vande Hei/NASA; 29: NASA; 30: Aubrey Gemignani/NASA; 31: NASA; 32 center: Robert Markowitz/NASA; 33 center: Tony Cenicola/The New York Times/Redux; 34–35: NASA/Science Source; 36: Alexander Gerst/ESA/NASA; 37 all: Ben Smegelsky/NASA; 38 left, 38 center left: NASA; 38 center right: Mikhail Metzel/AP Images; 38 right: Emmett Given/NASA; 39 left, 39 center: NASA; 39 right: Valery Sharifulin/TASS/Getty Images; 40–41, 42 graph paper: billnoll/Getty Images; 40 left: CSA/NASA; 40 right: Let's Talk Science/NASA; 42–43: Illustrations by Roger Zanni.

All other photos © Shutterstock.